Big Spider

Written by Teresa Heapy

Illustrated by Adrienne Kennaway

Once there was a very big spider.
He had a big day ahead.

2

3

First of all, Yellow Bird flew by.
"Special news!" she said. "There
will be a party in the North!"

A party! That sounded good!

Second of all, he met Tree Frog.
"Good news!" said Tree Frog.
"There will be a party in the South!"

Big Spider was getting very excited.

Third of all, he saw Bush Pig.
"Have you heard?" said Bush Pig.
"There will be a party in the East!"

Big Spider did not know what to do. Should he go to the party in the North? Or in the South instead? What about the party in the East?

Then he saw Monkey. Monkey bent down his head. "Come on!" he said. "We can catch a party in the West!"

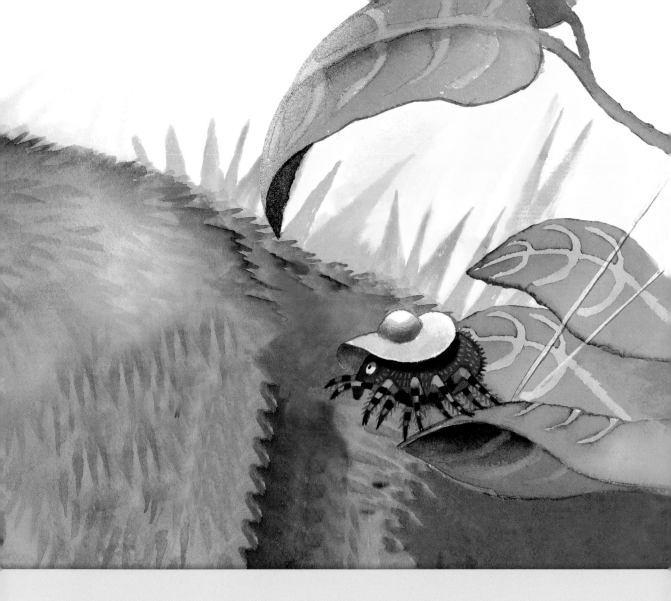

Big Spider nearly leapt in the air.
He was on a mission to party!

But Big Spider wanted to go to every party. He had to use his head.

He tied four strings around his belly.
He gave each animal a section of string.
"Stretch your string to the party!"
he said. "Tug when the party starts."

Off went the animals, clutching their strings.
"I shall watch for each tug and hear
about each party in turn," said Big Spider.

But all the parties started at once.
So all the animals pulled their strings
at the same time.

Big Spider got a shock! As the animals pulled harder his belly got smaller. And that is why spiders have long legs and tiny little bellies!